scribble my first ~~Coloring~~ BOOK

Advent Calendar

from 1 year

First english edition September 2024

This book belongs to:

_____

my own scribble

my own scribble

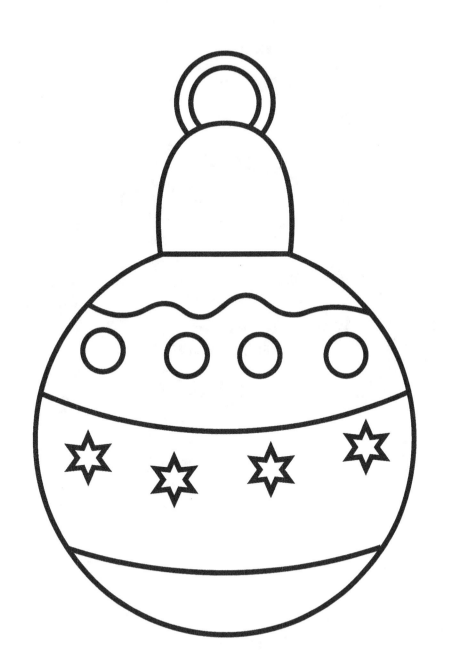

my own Scribble

my own Scribble

my own Scribble

my own Scribble

my own Scribble

my own Scribble

my own Scribble

my own Scribble

my own Scribble

my own Scribble

my own Scribble

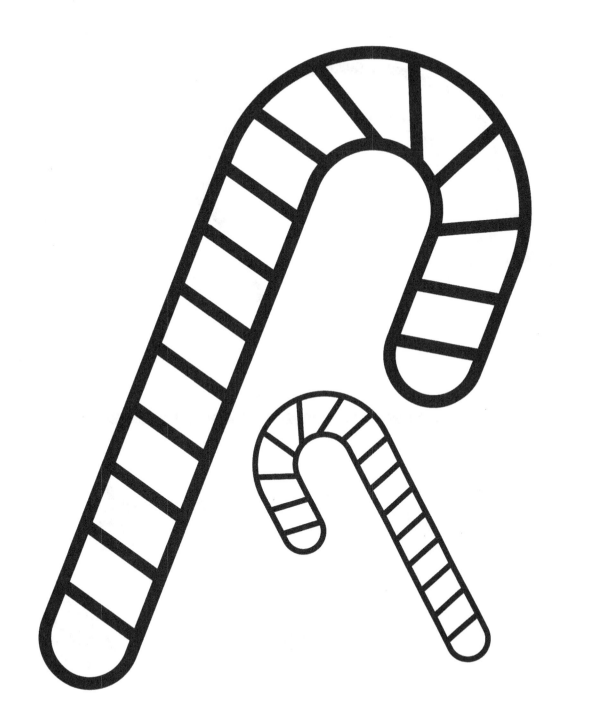

my own scribble

my own Scribble

my own Scribble

my own Scribble

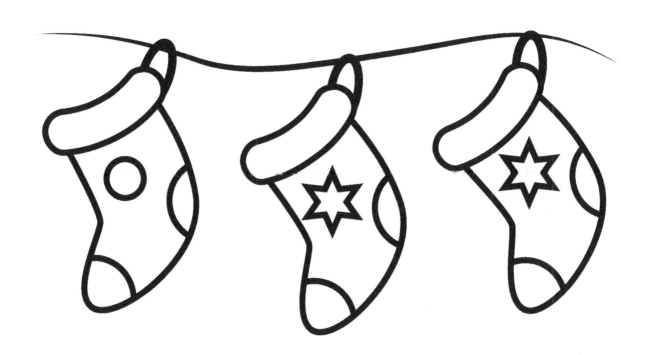

my own Scribble

my own scribble

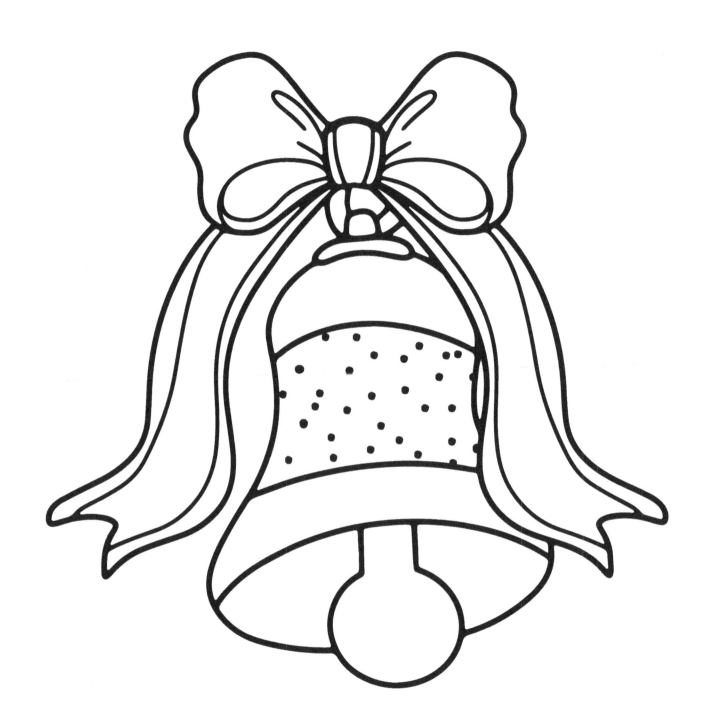

my own Scribble

my own scribble

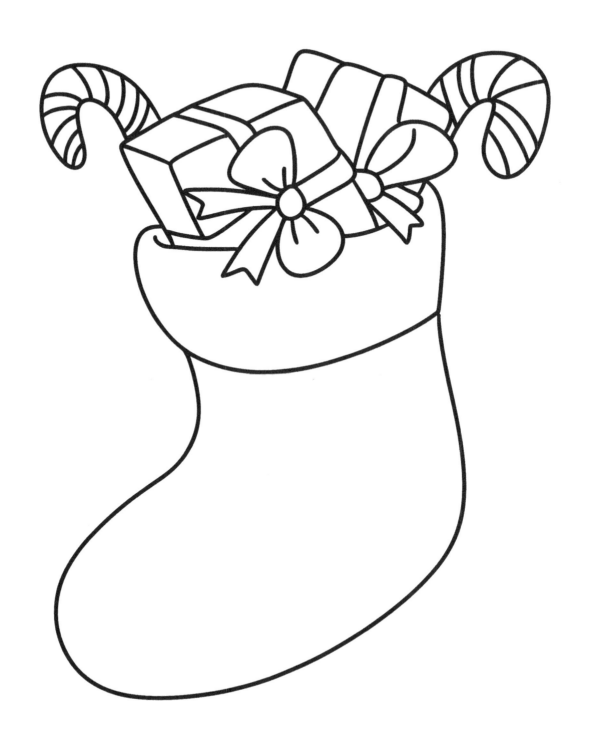

my own **scribble**

my own scribble

my own scribble

my own Scribble

Imprint

English-language first edition September 2024.

Sophia Mueller is represented by:
Tikva Verlag GmbH
Schillerstraße 26
79183 Waldkirch
Germany

I welcome questions, suggestions, and feedback at:
philipp@tikva-verlag.de

Feel free to leave me a review on Amazon.

ISBN: 9798339440581
Independently published

Made in the USA
Las Vegas, NV
25 November 2024